Sound of Living Waters

Song

BETTY PULKINGHAM

and

JEANNE HARPER

HODDER AND STOUGHTON
LONDON SYDNEY AUCKLAND TORONTO

Contents

Foreword

This handbook for the first volume of *Sound of Living Waters* is designed for groups whose leaders have the music edition. Suggestions for additional versions to songs, directions as to the manner of singing them, and topical indexes, therefore find no place here. We trust our readers will refer to the music edition for these, as also for the acknowledgements, though a list of the copyright permissions is included.

Sound of of Living Waters is a book with many fresh sounds reflecting the cascade of joyous praise, of awesome wonder, of sincerity and hope, which accompany the Holy Spirit's renewal in the Church today. It is not strictly speaking an innovative book; a great majority of the songs were chosen because of their proven usefulness in worship. In a sense our task as compilers has been not to choose, but to recognise what God seems already to have chosen. From the coasts of England, from the islands of New Zealand, from the expansive shores of America, the songs roll in as a powerful tide of praise to the Saviour. The ocean is deep and wide and so also is the musical scope of this book; it is not limited by period or style, not confined to youth or content with the old. Simply to turn a page may transport you from Handel to the sound of rock in 'Godspell'. We believe that such a mixture of sounds reflects the wideness of God's mercy — like the wideness of the sea. Certainly it reflects the breadth and variety of sources from which the music has been drawn, because in a real sense the book represents many voices in many lands.

This is not a collection of songs by 'experts' although Vaughan Williams and Bortniansky do have their say. So does a secretary named Sylvia, a young college student called Diane, and four-year-old David, son of one of the editors! The Holy Spirit gives songs as one means of encouraging the body of Christ and the book would make an interesting manual for studying the creative process. There are songs here which are 'open-ended': verses may be added spontaneously such as 'Thank you, Lord' and 'I will sing'. Time-honoured words may appear in new musical clothing: one such new hymn setting, 'On Jordan's bank' was the result of a parish choir rehearsal to prepare for the Feast-day of St. John the Baptist. The song-gifts of the Holy Spirit may be evidenced in interesting and varied ways. In one English parish a simple bright chorus, 'Thank you, thank you, Jesus' underwent a kind of metamorphosis: first, a member of the choir shared with the director his idea about the song ('I can hear it sung very slowly and worshipfully.') The director with some trepidation mentioned the seedling idea to the choir, and the following week a gifted young guitarist turned up with a unique reharmonisation of the song expressive of quiet awe and wonder. Yet another chorister contributed a verse of words and gradually a new song emerged — a composite of many small parts yet woven into one unique whole. 'The voice of God,' said the prophet Ezekiel, 'is as the sound of many waters'. One sound ... many waters.

So in the ebb and flow of music through the pages of *Sound of Living Waters* is to be found not only variety but a certain unity characterised by gentleness and peaceful praise. We hope you will peruse, enjoy and use it, and since praise pleases our Father, we are confident that he too will enjoy *Sound of Living Waters* — as you use it.

BETTY PULKINGHAM AND JEANNE HARPER
1975

1. Alleluia No.1

Don Fishel

Refrain
Alleluia, alleluia, give thanks to the risen Lord,
Alleluia, alleluia, give praise to his name.

1. Jesus is Lord of all the earth.
   He is the King of creation.

2. Spread the good news o'er all the earth.
   Jesus has died and has risen.

3. We have been crucified with Christ.
   Now we shall live for ever.

4. God has proclaimed the just reward,
   Life for all men, alleluia.

5. Come let us praise the living God,
   Joyfully sing to our Saviour.

2. The canticle of the gift

Refrain
O what a gift! What a wonderful gift!
Who can tell the wonders of the Lord?
Let us open our eyes, our ears, and our hearts;
  It is Christ the Lord, it is he!

1. In the stillness of the night
    When the world was asleep,
    The almighty Word leapt out.
    He came to Mary, he came to us,
    Christ came to the land of Galilee.
        Christ our Lord and our King!

2. On the night before he died
    It was Passover night,
    And he gathered his friends together.
    He broke the bread, he blessed the wine;
    It was the gift of his love and his life.
        Christ our Lord and our King!

3. On the hill of Calvary
    The world held its breath,
    For there for the world to see,
    God gave his Son, his very own Son
    For the love of you and me.
        Christ our Lord and our King!

4. Early on that morning
    When the guards were sleeping,
    Back to life came he!
    He conquered death, he conquered sin,
    But the vict'ry he gave to you and me!
        Christ our Lord and our King!

5. Some day with the saints
    We will come before our Father
    And then we will shout and dance and sing.
    For in our midst for our eyes to see
    Will be Christ our Lord and our King!
        Christ our Lord and our King!

3. Something in my heart

Anon.

Something in my heart like a stream running free
Makes me feel so happy, as happy as can be;
When I think of Jesus and what he's done for me,
Something in my heart like a stream running free.

4. Give me oil in my lamp

Anon.

1. Give me oil in my lamp, keep me burning.
    Give me oil in my lamp, I pray.
    Give me oil in my lamp, keep me burning,
    Keep me burning 'til the break of day.

Refrain
Sing hosanna, sing hosanna,
Sing hosanna to the King of kings!

2. Make me a fisher of men, keep me seeking...

3. Give me joy in my heart, keep me singing...

4. Give me love in my heart, keep me serving...

5.   Amazing grace

John Newton

1.   Amazing grace! How sweet the sound
           That saved a wretch like me.
    I once was lost, but now am found,
           Was blind, but now I see.

2.   'Twas grace that taught my heart to fear,
           And grace my fears relieved.
    How precious did that grace appear
           The hour I first believed.

3.   Through many dangers, toils and snares,
           I have already come;
    'Tis grace hath brought me safe thus far,
           And grace will lead me home.

4.   When we've been there ten thousand years,
           Bright shining as the sun,
    We've no less days to sing God's praise
           Than when we've first begun.

6. Oh! How good is the Lord

Anon.

Refrain
Oh! Oh! Oh! how good is the Lord. *Three times*
I never will forget what he has done for me.

1. He gives me salvation, how good is the Lord.
                                        Three times
   I never will forget what he has done for me.

2. He gives me his blessings...

3. He gives me his Spirit...

4. He gives me his healing...

5. He gives me his glory...

7.   I will sing, I will sing

Max Dyer

I will sing, I will sing a song unto the Lord. *Three times*
Alleluia, glory to the Lord.

Refrain
Allelu, alleluia, glory to the Lord. *Three times*
Alleluia, glory to the Lord.

Optional verses:

We will come, we will come as one before the Lord.
  Alleluia, glory to the Lord.

If the Son, if the Son shall make you free,
  You shall be free indeed.

They that sow in tears shall reap in joy.
  Alleluia, glory to the Lord.

Every knee shall bow and every tongue confess
  That Jesus Christ is Lord.

In his name, in his name we have the victory.
  Alleluia, glory to the Lord.

8.   # Let us give thanks

Brian Howard

Refrain
Let us give thanks
That our names are written,
Let us give thanks
That our names are written,
Written in the book of life,
Inscribed upon his palms,
Written in the book of life,
Inscribed upon his palms.

1.   Rejoice not that devils flee in his name.
   Rejoice not in the power that he gave;
   For he came to break the bonds of sin.
   Yes he did, he came to set us free, so freely we
                                 sing.

2.   For he came to give us life,
   That we might have it more abundantly;
   Came to break the power of sin, he did.
   Yes, he did, he came to set us free, so freely we
                                 sing.

3.   Let us give thanks,
   Thanks unto the Father,
   Thanks unto the Son,
   Thanks to the Holy Spirit,
   Our Lord God Three in One.

9.   Morning has broken

Eleanor Farjeon

1.   Morning has broken like the first morning;
        Blackbird has spoken like the first bird.
     Praise for the singing! Praise for the morning!
        Praise for them springing fresh from the word.

2.   Sweet the rain's new fall, sunlit from heaven,
        Like the first dew fall on the first grass.
     Praise for the sweetness of the wet garden,
        Sprung in completeness where his feet pass.

3.   Mine is the sunlight! Mine is the morning;
        Born of the one light Eden saw play.
     Praise with elation! Praise every morning
        God's re-creation of the new day.

10.   Rejoice in the Lord always

Anon.

Rejoice in the Lord always, and again I say rejoice.
Rejoice in the Lord always, and again I say rejoice.
Rejoice, rejoice, and again I say rejoice.
Rejoice, rejoice, and again I say rejoice.

11. Praise to the Lord

Joachim Neander

1. Praise to the Lord, the almighty, the King of
creation;
O my soul, praise him for he is thy health and
salvation;
Join the great throng,
Psaltery, organ and song,
Sounding in glad adoration.

2. Praise to the Lord, over all things he gloriously
reigneth;
Borne as on eagle wings, safely his saints he
sustaineth.
Hast thou not seen
How all thou needest hath been
Granted in what he ordaineth?

3. Praise to the Lord, who doth prosper thy way
and defend thee;
Surely his goodness and mercy shall ever attend
thee;
Ponder anew
What the almighty can do,
Who with his love doth befriend thee.

4. Praise to the Lord! O let all that is in me adore
him!
All that hath breath join with Abraham's seed to
adore him!
Let the 'Amen'
Sum all our praises again
Now as we worship before him.

12. Angel voices ever singing

Francis Pott

1. Angel voices ever singing
   Round thy throne of light,
Angel harps for ever ringing,
   Rest not day nor night;
Thousands only live to bless thee,
And confess thee
   Lord of might.

2. Thou who art beyond the farthest
   Mortal eye can scan.
Can it be that thou regardest
   Songs of sinful man?
Can we know that thou art near us
And wilt hear us?
   Yes, we can.

3. Yes, we know that thou rejoicest
   O'er each work of thine;
Thou didst ears and hands and voices
   For thy praise design;
Craftsman's art and music's measure
For thy pleasure
   All combine.

4. In thy house, great God, we offer
    Of thine own to thee;
And for thine acceptance proffer
    All unworthily,
Hearts and minds and hands and voices
In our choicest
    Psalmody.

5. Honour, glory, might, and merit
    Thine shall ever be,
Father, Son, and Holy Spirit,
    Blessed Trinity.
Of the best that thou hast given
Earth and heaven
    Render thee.

13.   This is the day

Anon.

1.   This is the day, this is the day
       that the Lord has made, that the Lord has made.

     We will rejoice, we will rejoice
       and be glad in it, and be glad in it.

     This is the day that the Lord has made.
     We will rejoice and be glad in it.

     This is the day that the Lord has made.

2.   This is the day when he rose again.

3.   This is the day when the Spirit came.

14.   Praise him

Anon.

1.   Praise him, praise him,
     Praise him in the morning,
     Praise him in the noontime,
     Praise him, praise him,
     Praise him when the sun goes down.

2.   Jesus..   4   Trust him.

3.   Love him.   5   Serve him.

15. Hallelujah! Jesus is Lord!

Mimi Armstrong Farra
Adapted from Rev. 7

Refrain
Hallelujah! Hallelujah! Hallelujah! Jesus is Lord!
Hallelujah! Hallelujah! Hallelujah! Jesus is King!

1. All gather round the throne of the Lamb,
    His praises sing throughout eternity.

2. Lift up your voice with the thousands who cry:
    'Worthy, worthy art thou, Lamb of God.'

3. Blessing and honour and glory and pow'r
    Be unto him for ever and ever.

4. All glory be to the one Triune God,
    The Father, Son, and the — Holy Spirit.

16. Jesus Christ is alive today

Anon.

Jesus Christ is alive today
[$_{We}^{I}$] know, [$_{We}^{I}$] know it's true.
Sovereign of the universe,
[$_{We}^{I}$] give him homage due.
Seated there at God's right hand,
[$_{We\,are}^{I\,am}$] with him in the promised land.
Jesus lives and reigns in [$_{you.}^{me.}$]
That's how I know it's true.

17.   O for a thousand tongues

Charles Wesley

1.   O for a thousand tongues to sing
       My great redeemer's praise,
     The glories of my God and King,
       The triumphs of his grace.

2.   Jesus! the name that charms our fears,
       That bids our sorrows cease;
     'Tis music in the sinner's ears,
       'Tis life, and health, and peace.

3.   He breaks the power of cancelled sin,
       He sets the prisoner free;
     His blood can make the foulest clean,
       His blood availed for me.

4.   He speaks, and listening to his voice,
       New life the dead receive,
     The mournful, broken hearts rejoice,
       The humble poor believe.

5.   Hear him, ye deaf; his praise, ye dumb,
       Your loosened tongues employ;
     Ye blind, behold your Saviour come,
       And leap, ye lame, for joy!

6.   My gracious master and my God
       Assist me to proclaim,
     To spread through all the earth abroad
       The honours of thy name.

18.   **Thank you, thank you, Jesus**

Anon.

1.   Thank you, thank you, Jesus.
     Thank you, thank you, Jesus.
     Thank you, thank you, Jesus, in my heart.
     Thank you, thank you, Jesus.
     Oh, thank you, thank you, Jesus.
     Thank you, thank you, Jesus, in my heart.

2.   You can't make me doubt him.
     You can't make me doubt him in my heart.
     You can't make me doubt him,
     I know too much about him.
     Thank you, thank you, Jesus, in my heart.

3.   I can't live without him.
     I can't live without him in my heart.
     I can't live without him,
     I know too much about him.
     Thank you, thank you, Jesus, in my heart.

4.   Glory, hallelujah!
     Glory, hallelujah, in my heart!
     Glory, hallelujah!
     Glory, hallelujah!
     Thank you, thank you, Jesus, in my heart!

19.   Holy, holy

1. Holy, holy, holy, holy.
    Holy, holy, Lord God Almighty;
    And we lift our hearts before you as a token of
                                        our love,
        Holy, holy, holy, holy.

2. Gracious Father, gracious Father,
    We're so glad to be your children, gracious
                                        Father;
    And we lift our heads before you as a token of
                                        our love,
        Gracious Father, gracious Father.

3. Precious Jesus, precious Jesus,
    We're so glad that you've redeemed us, precious
                                        Jesus,
    And we lift our hands before you as a token of
                                        our love,
        Precious Jesus, precious Jesus.

4. Holy Spirit, Holy Spirit,
    Come and fill our hearts anew, Holy Spirit,
    And we lift our voice before you as a token of our
                                        love,
        Holy Spirit, Holy Spirit.

5. Repeat verse 1.

6. Hallelujah, hallelujah, hallelujah, hallelujah,
    And we lift our hearts before you as a token of
                                        our love.
        Hallelujah, hallelujah.

20. Let all that is within me

Anon.

Let all that is within me cry, 'Holy.'
Let all that is within me cry, 'Holy.'
Holy, holy, holy is the Lamb that was slain.

Let all that is within me cry, 'Worthy'...
'Jesus'...
'Glory'...

21. Son of God

Oressa Wise

1. Son of God, Son of God,
    We come before you
    To love and adore you,
    Son of God.

2. Word of God, Word of God,
    We come to hear you,
    To always be near you,
    Word of God.

3. Lamb of God, Lamb of God,
    We come to bless you,
    To ever confess you,
    Lamb of God.

4. *Repeat verse* 1.

22. God himself is with us

Gerhardt Tersteegen

1. God himself is with us;
   Let us all adore him,
   And with awe appear before him.
   God is here within us:
   Soul in silence fear him,
   Humbly, fervently draw near him.
   Now his own who have known
   God, in worship lowly,
   Yield their spirits wholly.

2. Come, abide within me;
   Let my soul, like Mary,
   Be thine earthly sanctuary.
   Come, indwelling Spirit,
   With transfigured splendour;
   Love and honour will I render,
   Where I go here below,
   Let me bow before thee,
   Know thee, and adore thee.

3. Gladly we surrender
   Earth's deceitful treasures,
   Pride of life, and sinful pleasures:
   Gladly, Lord, we offer
   Thine to be for ever,
   Soul and life and each endeavour,
   Thou alone shalt be known
   Lord of all our being,
   Life's true way decreeing.

23.   We see the Lord

Anon.

We see the Lord,
We see the Lord,
And he is high and lifted up,
And his train fills the temple.
He is high and lifted up,
And his train fills the temple.
The angels cry, 'Holy',
The angels cry, 'Holy',
The angels cry, 'Holy is the Lord.'

24.   He is Lord

Anon.

He is Lord, he is Lord,
He is risen from the dead, and he is Lord.
Every knee shall bow,
Ever tongue confess
That Jesus Christ is Lord.

25. Alleluia

Anon.

1. Alleluia. *Eight times*
2. How I love him.
3. Blessed Jesus.
4. My Redeemer
5. Jesus is Lord.
6. Alleluia.

26. Father we adore you
(3-part round)

Terrye Coelho

Father, we adore you;
Lay our lives before you.
How we love you.

Jesus we adore you...

Spirit we adore you...

27.   Thank you, thank you, Jesus

Anon.

1. Thank you, thank you, Jesus.
   Thank you, thank you, Jesus.
   Oh, thank you, thank you, Jesus in my heart.
   Thank you, thank you, Jesus.
   Oh, thank you, thank you, Jesus.
   Oh, thank you, thank you, Jesus, in my heart.

2. Love you, love you, Jesus.
   Love you, love you, Jesus.
   Oh, love you, love you, Jesus in my heart...

3. Father, God almighty.
   Father, God almighty,
   Oh, Father, God almighty, take my heart...

4. Glory hallelujah!
   Glory hallelujah!
   Oh, glory hallelujah in my heart...

28. **Thou art worthy**

Pauline Michael Mills
and Tom Smail. Adapted from
Rev 4:11 and 5:9,10

1. Thou art worthy, thou art worthy,
      Thou art worthy, O Lord.
   Thou art worthy to receive glory,
      Glory and honour and power.
   For thou hast created, hast all things created,
      For thou hast created all things.
   And for thy pleasure they are created;
      Thou art worthy, O Lord.

2. Thou art worthy, thou art worthy,
      Thou art worthy, O Lamb.
   Thou art worthy to receive glory,
      And power at the Father's right hand.
   For thou hast redeemed us, hast ransomed and
                                    cleaned us
      By thy blood setting us free;
   In white robes arrayed us, kings and priests
                                    made us,
      And we are reigning in thee.

29.   Spirit of the living God

Daniel Iverson

Spirit of the living God, fall afresh on me.
Spirit of the living God, fall afresh on me.
Break me, melt me, mould me, fill me.
Spirit of the living God, fall afresh on me.

30.   Jesus, never have I heard a name

Anon.

Jesus, Jesus, Jesus,
Never have I heard a name that thrills my soul like
thine.
Jesus, Jesus, Jesus,
Oh what matchless grace that links that precious
name with mine.

31. All of my life

Germaine

Refrain
All of my life
I will sing praise
To my God.

1. For creation, praise;
   For salvation, praise;
   For all mankind, praise.

2. With your saints, sing praise;
   With the angels, praise;
   With all creatures, praise.

3. To the Father, praise;
   To the Son, sing praise;
   To the Spirit, praise.

32. Jesus, Jesus, wonderful Lord

Sylvia Lawton

1. Jesus, Jesus, wonderful Lord,
   Gently you touched me and made my life whole;
   How can I thank you except that I see
   Your way of life is truly for me?

2. Jesus, Jesus, take my life,
   Jesus, Jesus, I give to you
   All things, always yours to become.
   Jesus my Saviour, I will be thine.

3. Seeing, looking with new eyes;
   Loving, caring just as you do;
   Learning all things from your point of view;
   Lord Jesus Christ, your touch is so true.

33.   Spirit divine

Andrew Reed

1.   Spirit divine, attend our prayers,
      And make this house thy home;
   Descend with all thy gracious powers,
      O come, great Spirit, come!

2.   Come as the light; to us reveal
      Our emptiness and woe,
   And lead us in those paths of life
      Whereon the righteous go.

3.   Come as the fire, and purge our hearts
      Like sacrificial flame;
   Let our whole soul an offering be
      To our redeemer's name.

4.   Come as the dove, and spread thy wings,
      The wings of peaceful love;
   And let thy Church on earth become
      Blest as the Church above.

5.   Spirit divine, attend our prayers;
      Make a lost world thy home;
   Descend with all thy gracious powers;
      O come, great Spirit, come!

34. I want to walk as a child of the light

Kathleen Thomerson

1. I want to walk as a child of the light.
   I want to follow Jesus.
   God set the stars to give light to the world.
   The star of my life is Jesus.

Refrain
In him there is no darkness at all,
  The night and the day are both alike.
The Lamb is the light of the city of God.
  Shine in my heart, Lord Jesus.

2. I want to see the brightness of God.
   I want to look at Jesus.
   Clear sun of righteousness, shine on my path,
   And show me the way to the Father.

3. I'm looking for the coming of Christ.
   I want to be with Jesus.
   When we have run with patience the race,
   We shall know the joy of Jesus.

35.   In Christ there is no east or west

John Oxenham

1.   In Christ there is no east or west,
         In him no south or north,
      But one great fellowship of love
         Throughout the whole wide earth.

2.   In him shall true hearts everywhere
         Their high communion find;
      His service is the golden cord
         Close binding all mankind.

3.   Join hands then, brothers of the faith,
         Whate'er your race may be;
      Who serves my Father as a son
         Is surely kin to me.

4.   In Christ now meet both east and west,
         In him meet south and north.
      All Christly souls are one in him
         Throughout the whole wide earth.

36. Lord, I want to be a Christian

American folk hymn

1. Lord, I want to be a Christian,
   In-a my heart, in-a my heart.
   Lord, I want to be a Christian,
   In-a my heart.
   In-a my heart, in-a my heart,
   Lord, I want to be a Christian in-a my heart.

2. Lord, I want to be more loving...

3. Lord, I want to be like Jesus...

4. Lord, I want to praise you freely...

37.   Day by day

Richard of Chichester
and Jeanne Harper

1. Day by day, dear Lord, of thee three things I
                                            pray:

>   To see thee more clearly,
>   To love thee more dearly,
>   To follow thee more nearly day by day.

2. Day by day, dear Lord, of thee three things I
                                            pray:

>   To trust thee more fully,
>   To leave things more wholly,
>   To lean on thee securely day by day.

38.   Day by day

Richard of Chichester

>   Day by day,
>   O dear Lord, three things I pray:
>>   To see thee more clearly,
>>   Love thee more dearly,
>>   Follow thee more nearly,
>   Day by day.

39. Reach out and touch the Lord

Bill Harmon

Reach out and touch the Lord as he goes by.
You'll find he's not too busy to hear your heart's cry.
He's passing by this moment your needs to supply.
Reach out and touch the Lord as he goes by.

40. I want to live for Jesus every day

Anon.

1.   I want to live for Jesus every day.
     I want to live for Jesus, come what may.
     Take the world and all its pleasure,
     I've got a more enduring treasure.
     I want to live for Jesus every day.

2.   I'm gonna' live for Jesus every day...

41. He shall teach you all things

He shall teach you all things,
   He shall teach you all things,
And bring all things to your remembrance,
   And bring all things to your remembrance.

42. Kum ba yah

('Come by here')

Traditional
spiritual

1. Kum ba yah, my Lord, Kum ba yah,
    Kum ba yah, my Lord, Kum ba yah;
    Kum ba yah, my Lord, Kum ba yah,
       O Lord, Kum ba yah.

2. Someone's crying, Lord, Kum ba yah...

3. Someone's singing, Lord, Kum ba yah...

4. Someone's praying, Lord, Kum ba yah...

43. O Breath of Life

Bessie Porter Head

1. O Breath of Life, come sweeping through us,
       Revive thy Church with life and power.
    O Breath of Life, come, cleanse, renew us,
       And fit thy Church to meet this hour.

2. O Wind of God, come bend us, break us,
       Till humbly we confess our need:
    Then in thy tenderness re-make us,
       Revive, restore; for this we plead.

3. O Breath of Love, come breathe within us,
       Renewing thought and will and heart;
    Come, love of Christ, afresh to win us,
       Revive thy Church in every part.

4. Revive us, Lord! Is zeal abating
       While harvest fields are vast and white?
    Revive us, Lord, the world is waiting,
       Equip thy Church to spread the light.

44. Lord of all hopefulness

Jan Struther

1. Lord of all hopefulness, Lord of all joy,
    Whose trust, ever childlike, no cares could des-
    troy,
    Be there at our waking, and give us, we pray,
    Your bliss in our hearts, Lord, at the break of the
    day.

2. Lord of all eagerness, Lord of all faith,
    Whose strong hands were skilled at the plane and
    the lathe,
    Be there at our labours, and give us, we pray,
    Your strength in our hearts, Lord, at the noon of
    the day.

3. Lord of all kindliness, Lord of all grace,
    Your hands swift to welcome, your arms to
    embrace,
    Be there at our homing, and give us, we pray,
    Your love in our hearts, Lord, at the eve of the
    day.

4. Lord of all gentleness, Lord of all calm,
    Whose voice is contentment, whose presence is
    balm,
    Be there at our sleeping, and give us, we pray,
    Your peace in our hearts, Lord, at the end of the
    day.

45. & 46.   At the name of Jesus

Caroline M. Noel

1. At the name of Jesus
   Every knee shall bow,
   Every tongue confess him
   King of glory now.
   'Tis the Father's pleasure
   We should call him Lord,
   Who from the beginning
   Was the mighty Word.

2. Humbled for a season,
   To receive a name
   From the lips of sinners,
   Unto whom he came,
   Faithfully he bore it,
   Spotless to the last,
   Brought it back victorious,
   When from death he passed.

3. Bore it up triumphant,
   With its human light,
   Through all ranks of creatures,
   To the central height,
   To the throne of Godhead,
   To the Father's breast;
   Filled it with the glory
   Of that perfect rest.

4. In your hearts enthrone him,
        There let him subdue
    All that is not holy,
        All that is not true:
    Crown him as your captain
        In temptation's hour;
    Let his will enfold you
        In its light and power.

5. Brothers, this Lord Jesus
        Shall return again,
    With his Father's glory
        O'er the earth to reign;
    For all wreaths of empire
        Meet upon his brow,
    And our hearts confess him
        King of glory now.

47.   I want to walk with Jesus Christ

St. Paul's Erith
1964 House Party

1.   I want to walk with Jesus Christ,
        All the days I live of this life on earth,
    To give to him complete control
        Of body and of soul.

Refrain
Follow him, follow him, yield your life to him,
  He has conquered death, he is King of kings.
Accept the joy which he gives to those
  Who yield their lives to him.

2.   I want to learn to speak to him,
        To pray to him, confess my sin,
    To open my life and let him in,
        For joy will then be mine.

3.   I want to learn to speak of him,
        My life must show that he lives in me.
    My deeds, my thoughts, my words must speak
        All of his love for me.

4.   I want to learn to read his word,
        For this is how I know the way
    To live my life as pleases him,
        In holiness and joy.

5.   O Holy Spirit of the Lord,
        Enter now into this heart of mine,
    Take full control of my selfish will
        And make me wholly thine.

48. How sweet the name of Jesus sounds

John Newton

1. How sweet the name of Jesus sounds
        In a believer's ear!
    It soothes his sorrows, heals his wounds,
        And drives away his fear.

2. It makes the wounded spirit whole,
        And calms the troubled breast;
    'Tis manna to the hungry soul,
        And to the weary rest.

3. Dear name, the rock on which I build,
        My shield and hiding place,
    My never-failing treasury, filled
        With boundless stores of grace.

4. Jesus! My Shepherd, Brother, Friend,
        My Prophet, Priest, and King,
    My Lord, my life, my way, my end,
        Accept the praise I bring.

5. Weak is the effort of my heart,
        And cold my warmest thought;
    But when I see thee as thou art,
        I'll praise thee as I ought.

6. Till then I would thy love proclaim
        With every fleeting breath;
    And may the music of thy name
        Refresh my soul in death.

49. Here comes Jesus

Anon.

Here comes Jesus, see him walking on the water,
   He'll lift you up and he'll help you to stand.
Here comes Jesus, he's the master of the waves that
   roll.
   Here comes Jesus, he'll make you whole.

*Repeat in ascending keys, ending with the following (extra)
words:*

Here comes Jesus, he'll save your soul.

50. Silver and gold have I none

Anon.

Verse
Peter and John went to pray,
   they met a lame man on the way.
He asked for alms and held out his palms,
   and this is what Peter did say:

Refrain
'Silver and gold have I none,
   but such as I have give I thee.
In the name of Jesus Christ
   of Nazareth, rise up and walk!'

He went walking and leaping and praising God,
   walking and leaping and praising God.
'In the name of Jesus Christ
   of Nazareth, rise up and walk.'

51.   **There is a balm in Gilead**

North American spiritual

Refrain
There is a balm in Gilead
   to make the wounded whole.
There is a balm in Gilead
   to heal the sin-sick soul.

1.   Sometimes I feel discouraged,
      and think my work's in vain,
   but then the Holy Spirit
      revives my soul again.

2.   If you cannot sing like angels,
      if you cannot preach like Paul,
   you can tell the love of Jesus
      and say he died for all.

52.   Dear Lord and Father

John Greenleaf Whittier

1.   Dear Lord and Father of mankind,
         Forgive our foolish ways!
     Reclothe us in our rightful mind;
         In purer lives thy service find,
     In deeper rev'rence praise.

2.   In simple trust like theirs who heard,
         Beside the Syrian sea,
     The gracious calling of the Lord,
         Let us like them, without a word,
     Rise up and follow thee.

3.   O sabbath rest by Galilee!
         O calm of hills above,
     Where Jesus knelt to share with thee
         The silence of eternity,
     Interpreted by love.

4.   With that deep hush subduing all
         Our words and works that drown
     The tender whisper of thy call,
         As noiseless let thy blessing fall
     As fell thy manna down.

5.   Drop thy still dews of quietness
         Till all our strivings cease:
     Take from our souls the strain and stress,
         And let our ordered lives confess
     The beauty of thy peace.

6.   Breathe through the heats of our desire
         Thy coolness and thy balm;
     Let sense be dumb, let flesh retire;
         Speak through the earthquake, wind and fire,
     O still small voice of calm.

53. The bell song

Symphony of souls

1. You gotta have love in your heart.
    You gotta have love in your heart.
    You knew it was Jesus right from the start
    You gotta have love in your heart.

2. You gotta have peace on your mind.
    You knew it was Jesus there all the time.

3. You gotta have joy in your soul.
    The love of Jesus will make you whole.

4. La la la la...

54. By your stripes

Pamela Greenwood

By your stripes, Lord, I'm healed, hallelujah!
In your word it is revealed, hallelujah!
Yes, you bore it all for me, on the cross of Calvary
So that now I can go free, hallelujah!

55.   Alleluia! sing to Jesus

William Dix

1.   Alleluia! Sing to Jesus!
    His the sceptre, his the throne;
  Alleluia! His the triumph,
    His the victory alone;
  Hark! The songs of peaceful Zion
    Thunder like a mighty flood;
  Jesus out of every nation
    Hath redeemed us by his blood.

2.   Alleluia! Not as orphans
    Are we left in sorrow now;
  Alleluia! He is near us,
    Faith believes, nor questions how:
  Though the cloud from sight received him,
    When the forty days were o'er,
  Shall our hearts forget his promise,
    'I am with you evermore'?

3.   Alleluia! Bread of heaven,
    Thou on earth our food, our stay!
  Alleluia! Here the sinful
    Flee to thee from day to day:
  Intercessor, friend of sinners,
    Earth's redeemer, plead for me,
  Where the songs of all the sinless
    Sweep across the crystal sea.

4. Alleluia! King eternal,
   Thee the Lord of lords we own:
   Alleluia! Born of Mary,
   Earth thy footstool, heav'n thy throne
   Thou within the veil hast entered,
   Robed in flesh, our great high priest
   Thou on earth both priest and victim
   In the eucharistic feast.

5. Alleluia! Sing to Jesus!
   His the sceptre, his the throne;
   Alleluia! His the triumph,
   His the victory alone;
   Hark! the songs of holy Zion
   Thunder like a mighty flood;
   Jesus out of every nation
   Hath redeemed us by his blood.

56. Blow, thou cleansing wind

Alan Teage

1. Blow, thou cleansing wind from heaven,
    Burn, thou fire, within our hearts.
Spirit of the Lord, possess us,
    Fill our lives in every part.
Mind of Christ, be thou our ruler.
    Word of truth, be thou our guide;
Leave no part of us unhallowed.
    Come, O come in us abide.

2. Fill thy Church, inspire and strengthen,
    Chasten, mould, empower and lead.
Make us one, and make us joyful,
    Give us grace for every need.
Be our life, build firm thy kingdom.
    Be our strength, who are but frail.
Then indeed against us never
    Shall the gates of hell prevail.

3. Win the world! Baptize the nations!
    Open every blinded eye.
Leave no sinner unconvicted;
    Leave no soul untouched and dry.
Conquering love, take thou the kingdom,
    Rule thou over all our days;
Then in glory and rejoicing
    Earth shall echo with thy praise.

57. Jesus

Debby Kerner

1. Jesus.   *Five times*
2. He died.
3. He rose.
4. He lives.
5. We live through him.
6. Jesus.

58. Seek ye first
(2-part round)

Karen Lafferty

Seek ye first the kingdom of God,
  And his righteousness,
And all these things shall be added unto you;
  Allelu, alleluia.

Alleluia, alleluia, alleluia,
  Allelu, alleluia.

59. Fear not! rejoice and be glad

Priscilla Wright
Adapted from Joel 2:21 - 27

Refrain
Fear not, rejoice and be glad,
The Lord hath done a great thing;
Hath poured out his Spirit on all mankind,
On those who confess his name.

1. The fig tree is budding, the vine beareth fruit,
   The wheat fields are golden with grain,
   Thrust in the sickle, the harvest is ripe,
   The Lord has given us rain.

2. Ye shall eat in plenty and be satisfied,
   The mountains will drip with sweet wine,
   My children shall drink of the fountain of life,
   My children will know they are mine.

3. My people shall know that I am the Lord,
   Their shame I have taken away.
   My Spirit will lead them together again,
   My Spirit will show them the way.

4. My children shall dwell in a body of love,
   A light to the world they will be:
   Life shall come forth from the Father above,
   My body will set mankind free.

60. God is building a house

Anon.
Verses 2.3.4 Hong Sit

1. God is building a house, God is building a house,
    God is building a house that will stand.
    He is building by his plan
        With the lively stones of man,
    God is building a house that will stand.

2. God is building a house, God is building a house,
    God is building a house that will stand.
    With apostles, prophets, pastors,
        With evangelists and teachers,
    God is building a house that will stand.

3. Christ is head of this house, Christ is head of this
                                            house,
    Christ is head of this house that will stand.
    He abideth in its praise,
        Will perfect it in its ways,
    Christ is head of this house that will stand.

4. We are part of this house, we are part of this
                                            house,
    We are part of this house that will stand.
    We are called from every nation
        To enjoy his full salvation,
    We are part of this house that will stand.

61. The kingdom of God

Brian Howard

1. The kingdom of God is neither lo here, nor lo
there,
No, the kingdom is among us.

2. The victory of God is neither lo here, nor lo
there,
No, the victory is among us.

3. The power of God is neither lo here, nor lo
there,
No, the power is among us.

4. The Spirit of God was not lost after Pentecost,
No, the Spirit is among us.

5. The Prince of peace has not gone away, he won't
let you stray,
No, the Prince of peace is among us.

6. The joy of the Lord is like a singing lark, deep
within your heart,
Let it flow so freely among us.

What a great thing it is

Ray Repp

Refrain
What a great thing it is, and
oh, how pleasant it can be for
　　all God's people
　　to live together in peace. So
now tell everyone you meet of the
joy that we were meant to see when
　　all God's people,
　　live together in peace.

1.　The Lord gave everyone a law
　　　that we should
　　love and follow every call from him.
　　　Love and follow every
　　　call from him.

2.　The Father promised us a home
　　　where we could
　　live together as a family.
　　　Live together as a
　　　family.

3.　Brothers, sisters are we all
　　　because we're
　　made as equal in the sight of God,
　　　made as equal in the
　　　sight of God.

4.　All you children of the Lord
　　　sing out and
　　praise our God for all eternity.
　　　Praise our God for all e-
　　　-ternity.

63.   **I am the bread of life**

1.   I am the bread of life;
He who/ comes to me shall not hunger;
He who be/lieves in me shall not thirst.
No-one can come to me
Un/ less the Father draw him.

Refrain
And I will raise him up *Repeat*
And I will raise him up on the last day.

2.   The bread that I will give
Is my/ flesh for the life of the world
And he who/ eats of this bread,
He shall live for ever.

3.   Un/ less you eat
Of the/ flesh of the Son of man
And/ drink of his blood *Repeat*
You shall/ not have life within you.

4.   I am the resurrection,
I am the life.
He who be/ lieves in me,
Even if he die,
He shall live for ever.

5.   Yes/ Lord, we believe
That/ you are the Christ,
The / Son of God
Who has come
In/ to the world.

64.   Oh, the blood of Jesus

Anon.

1. Oh, the blood of Jesus, *Three times*
   It washes white as snow.

2. Oh, the word of Jesus,
   It cleanses white as snow.

3. Oh, the love of Jesus,
   It makes his body whole.

65.   At the cross

Sankey

At the cross, at the cross where I first saw the light,
And the burden of my heart rolled away,
It was there by faith I received my sight,
And now I am happy all the day.

66.   A new commandment

Anon.

A new commandment I give unto you,
    that you love one another, as I have loved you,
    that you love one another, as I have loved you.
By this shall all men know you are my disciples
    if you have love one to another.
By this shall all men know you are my disciples
    if you have love one to another.

57. God and men at table are sat down

Robert Stamps

1. O welcome, all ye noble saints of old
   As now before your very eyes unfold
   The wonders all so long ago foretold:
      God and man at table are sat down.

2. Elders, martyrs, all are falling down,
   Prophets, patriarchs are gathering round.
   What angels longed to see now man has found.
      God and man at table are sat down.

3. Who is this who spreads the victory feast?
   Who is this who makes our warring cease?
   Jesus, risen Saviour, Prince of Peace.
      God and man at table are sat down.

4. Beggars, lame and harlots also here;
   Repentant publicans are drawing near,
   Wayward sons come home without a fear,
      God and man at table are sat down.

5. Worship in the presence of the Lord
   With joyful songs and hearts in one accord,
   And let our host at table be adored.
      God and man at table are sat down.

6. When at last this earth shall pass away,
   When Jesus and his bride are one to stay,
   The feast of love is just begun that day,
      God and man at table are sat down.

68.   # Glory be to Jesus

Tr. Edward Caswall

1. Glory be to Jesus,
    Who in bitter pains
Poured for me the life-blood
    From his sacred veins!

2. Grace and life eternal
    In that blood I find,
Blest be his compassion
    Infinitely kind!

3. Blest through endless ages
    Be the precious stream
Which from sin and sorrow
    Doth the world redeem!

4. Oft as earth exulting
    Wafts its praise on high,
Angel-hosts rejoicing,
    Make their glad reply.

5. Lift ye then your voices;
    Swell the mighty flood;
Louder still and louder
    Praise the precious blood.

69. We really want to thank you, Lord

Ed. Baggett

Refrain
We really want to thank you, Lord.
We really want to bless your name.
Hallelujah! Jesus is our king!

1. We thank you, Lord, for your gift to us,
        Your life so rich beyond compare,
    The gift of your body here on earth
        Of which we sing and share.

2. We thank you, Lord, for our life together,
        To live and move in the love of Christ,
    Tenderness which sets us free
        To serve you with our lives.

70.   This is my commandment

Anon.

This is my commandment that you love one another,
That your joy may be full.
This is my commandment that you love one another,
That your joy may be full
That your joy may be full,
That your joy may be full;
This is my commandment that you love one another
That your joy may be full.

71.   # The king of love

H.W.Baker

1.   The king of love my shepherd is,
       Whose goodness faileth never;
    I nothing lack if I am his,
       And he is mine for ever.

2.   Where streams of living water flow,
       My ransomed soul he leadeth,
    And where the verdant pastures grow,
       With food celestial feedeth.

3.   Perverse and foolish oft I strayed,
       But yet in love he sought me,
    And on his shoulder gently laid,
       And home, rejoicing, brought me.

4.   In death's dark vale I fear no ill
       With thee, dear Lord, beside me;
    Thy rod and staff my comfort still,
       Thy cross before to guide me.

5.   Thou spread'st a table in my sight;
       Thy unction grace bestoweth;
    And O what transport of delight
       From thy pure chalice floweth!

6.   And so through all the length of days
       Thy goodness faileth never:
    Good shepherd, may I sing thy praise
       Within thy house for ever.

72. Glorious things of thee are spoken

John Newton

1.   Glorious things of thee are spoken,
        Zion, city of our God.
    He whose word cannot be broken,
        Formed thee for his own abode:
    On the rock of ages founded,
        What can shake thy sure repose?
    With salvation's walls surrounded,
        Thou may'st smile at all thy foes.

2.   See the streams of living waters,
        Springing from eternal love,
    Well supply thy sons and daughters,
        And all fear of want remove:
    Who can faint while such a river
        Ever flows their thirst to assuage?
    Grace which like the Lord, the giver,
        Ever flows from age to age.

3.   Round each habitation hovering,
        See the cloud and fire appear!
    For a glory and a covering
        Showing that the Lord is near:
    He who gives them daily manna,
        He who listens when they cry:
    Let him hear the loud hosanna,
        Rising to his throne on high.

4. Saviour, since of Zion's city
    I through grace a member am,
Let the world deride or pity,
    I will glory in thy name;
Fading is the worldling's pleasure,
    All his boasted pomp and show;
Solid joys and lasting treasure
    None but Zion's children know.

5. Blest inhabitants of Zion;
    Washed in the Redeemer's blood!
Jesus, whom their souls rely on,
    Makes them kings and priests to God.
'Tis his love his people raises
    Over self to reign as kings:
And as priests, his solemn praises
    Each for a thank-offering brings.

There is no song 73

74. God has called you

Diane Davis

1. God has called (name), he will not fail (him,her).
   God has called (name), he will not fail (him,her).
   God has called (name), he will not fail (him,her),
   So trust in God and obey him.

2. God has called you, he will not fail you.
   So trust in God and obey him.

3. God has called us, we will not fail him.
   So trust in God and obey him.

75. How firm a foundation

John Rippon

1. How firm a foundation, ye saints of the Lord,
   Is laid for your faith in his excellent word!
   What more can he say than to you he hath said,
   To you that for refuge to Jesus have fled?

2. 'Fear not, I am with thee; O be not dismayed!
   For I am thy God, and will still give thee aid;
   I'll strengthen thee, help thee, and cause thee to
                                            stand,
   Upheld by my righteous, omnipotent hand.

3. 'When through the deep waters I call thee to go,
   The rivers of woe shall not thee overflow;
   For I will be with thee, thy troubles to bless,
   And sanctify to thee thy deepest distress.

4. 'When through fiery trials thy pathway shall lie,
   My grace, all-sufficient, shall be thy supply;
   The flame shall not hurt thee; I only design
   Thy dross to consume, and thy gold to refine.

5. 'The soul that to Jesus has fled for repose,
   I will not, I will not desert to his foes;
   That soul, though all hell shall endeavour to shake,
   I'll never, no never, no never forsake.'

Complete in him

Anon.

1. The fullness of the Godhead bodily
    Dwelleth in my Lord.
   The fullness of the Godhead bodily
    Dwelleth in my Lord.
   The fullness of the Godhead bodily
    Dwelleth in my Lord
   And we are complete in him.

Refrain
   Complete, complete,
    Complete in him,
   We are complete in him.

2. It's not by works of righteousness
    But by his grace alone...
   That we are complete in him.

3. There's nothing more that I can do
    For Jesus did it all...
   And we are complete in him.

77. The Holy Ghost Medley

Arr. Betty Pulkingham

Jesus gave her water
That was not from the well,
Gave her living water
And sent her forth to tell:
She went away singing,
And came back bringing
Others for the water
That was not from the well.

Drinking at the springs of living water,
Happy now am I, my soul is satisfied,
Drinking at the springs of living water,
What a wonderful and bounteous supply.

Spring up, O well, within my soul.
Spring up, O well, and overflow;
Spring up, O well, flow out through me.
Spring up, O well, set others free.

1.   There's a river of life flowing out through me,
        It makes the lame to walk and the blind to see,
     Opens prison doors, sets the captives free,
        There's a river of life flowing out through me.

2. There's a fountain flowing from the Saviour's side,
   All my sins forgiven in that precious tide.
   Jesus paid the price when for me he died.
   There's a fountain flowing from the Saviour's
   side.

3. There's a risen Saviour at the Father's throne,
   Ever interceding for his very own,
   Pouring down the blessings that are his alone.
   There's a risen Saviour at the Father's throne.

4. There's a holy comforter who's sent from heaven,
   All the glorious gifts are his, and have been
   given,
   He'll /show us more of Jesus 'til the veil is riven.
   There's a holy comforter who's sent from
   heaven.

5. There's a land of rest that we may enter now,
   Freed from all our works and freed from
   Satan's power,
   Just /resting in the Lord each moment and each
   hour.
   There's a land of rest that we may enter now.

6. There's a full salvation wrought for you and me,
   From /faith to faith and /glory to glory
   e /ternally,
   O/Lord, just take this life and let me live for thee.
   There's a full salvation wrought for you and me.

78.   I have decided to follow Jesus

Paul Smith

1. I have decided to follow Jesus.
    I have decided to follow Jesus.
    I have decided to follow Jesus.
        No turning back, no turning back.

2. The world behind me, the cross before me.
        No turning back, no turning back.

3. Tho' none go with me, still I will follow.
        No turning back, no turning back.

4. Where Jesus leads me, I'll surely follow.
        No turning back, no turning back.

5. Sing glory, glory and hallelujah.
        No turning back, no turning back.

79. See the conqueror mounts in triumph

Christopher Wordsworth

1. See the conqueror mounts in triumph,
   See the King in royal state,
   Riding on the clouds, his chariot,
   To his heavenly palace gate!
      Hark! the choirs of angel voices
      Joyful alleluias sing.
      And the portals high are lifted
      To receive their heavenly King.

2. He who on the cross did suffer,
   He who from the grave arose,
   He has vanquished sin and Satan:
   He by death has spoiled his foes.
      While he lifts his hands in blessing,
      He is parted from his friends;
      While their eager eyes behold him,
      He upon the clouds ascends.

3. Thou hast raised our human nature
   On the clouds to God's right hand:
   There we sit in heavenly places,
   There with thee in glory stand.
      Jesus reigns, adored by angels;
      Man with God is on the throne;
      Mighty Lord, in thine ascension,
      We by faith behold our own.

80.   Hail, thou once despised Jesus

John Blackwell and
Martin Madan

1   Hail, thou once despised Jesus!
Hail, thou Galilean King!
Thou didst suffer to release us;
Thou didst free salvation bring.
    Hail, thou universal Saviour,
    Bearer of our sin and shame.
    By thy merit we find favour:
    Life is given through thy name.

2.   Paschal Lamb, by God appointed,
All our sins on thee were laid:
By almighty love anointed,
Thou hast full atonement made.
    All thy people are forgiven
    Through the virtue of thy blood:
    Opened is the gate of heaven,
    Peace is made 'twixt man and God.

3.   Jesus, hail! enthroned in glory,
There for ever to abide;
All the heavenly hosts adore thee,
Seated at thy Father's side.
    There for sinners thou art pleading:
    There thou dost our place prepare;
    Ever for us interceding,
    Till in glory we appear.

4.   Worship, honour, power, and blessing
       Thou art worthy to receive:
       Highest praises, without ceasing,
       Meet it is for us to give.
          Help, ye bright angelic spirits,
          Bring your sweetest, noblest lays;
          Help to sing our Saviour's merits,
          Help to chant Emmanuel's praise!

81.   He signed my deed

Anon

He signed my deed with his atoning blood,
He ever lives to make his promise good.
Though all the hosts of hell march in to make a
                            second claim,
They'll all march out at the mention of his name.
                          Three times.

82.

Jesus is Lord

David J. Mansell

1. 'Jesus is Lord!' Creation's voice proclaims it,
For by his power each tree and flower was
planned and made.
'Jesus is Lord!' The universe declares it.
Sun, moon and stars in heaven cry 'Jesus is Lord!'

    Refrain
    Jesus is Lord! Jesus is Lord!
    Praise him with 'Hallelujahs' for Jesus is Lord!

2. Jesus is Lord! Yet from his throne eternal
In flesh he came to die in pain on Calvary's tree.
Jesus is Lord! From him all life proceeding,
Yet gave his life a ransom thus setting us free.

3. Jesus is Lord! O'er sin the mighty conqueror,
From death he rose and all his foes shall own his
name.
Jesus is Lord! God sends his Holy Spirit
To show by works of power that Jesus is Lord.

83.

The joy of the Lord

Anon.

1.   The joy of the Lord is my strength. *Four times*

Refrain
A-ha-ha-ha... *Ls. 1-3*
The joy of the Lord is my strength.

2.   If you want joy you must sing for it,
     If you want joy you must shout for it;
     If you want joy you must jump for it.
     The joy of the Lord is my strength.

3.   The word of faith is nigh thee, even in thy mouth.
                                      Three times

     The joy of the Lord is my strength.

84. I heard the Lord

Jacob Krieger

1.   I heard the Lord
     Call my name,
  Listen close,
     You'll hear the same.
  I heard the Lord
     Call my name,
  Listen close,
     You'll hear the same.
  I heard the Lord
     Call my name,
  Listen close,
     You'll hear the same.
  Take his hand
  We are glory bound.

2.   His word is love,
     Love's his word,
  That's the message
     That I heard.
  Take his hand,
  We are glory bound.

  Place your hand in his and
     You will know
  He will show you
     Where to go.

3.   I felt his love
      From above
   Settle on me
      Like a dove.
   Take his hand,
   We are glory bound.

4.   And to the Father
      All your days
   With the Son
      And Spirit praise.
   Take his hand,
   We are glory bound.

   Place your hand in his and
   You will know,
   He will show you
      Where to go.

5.   *Repeat verse 1.*

85.   And can it be?

Charles Wesley

1. And can it be that I should gain
     An interest in the Saviour's blood?
   Died he for me, who caused his pain?
     For me, who him to death pursued?
   Amazing love! how can it be
   That thou, my God, shouldst die for me?

2. 'Tis mystery all! th'immortal dies!
     Who can explore his strange design?
   In vain the firstborn seraph tries
     To sound the depths of love divine!
   'Tis mercy all! let earth adore,
   Let angel minds inquire no more.

3. He left his father's throne above,
     So free, so infinite his grace;
   Emptied himself of all but love,
     And bled for Adam's helpless race;
   'Tis mercy all, immense and free;
   For, O my God, it found out me.

4. Long my imprisoned spirit lay
     Fast bound in sin and nature's night;
   Thine eye diffused a quickening ray,
     I woke, the dungeon flamed with light;
   My chains fell off, my heart was free;
   I rose, went forth, and followed thee.

5. No condemnation now I dread;
     Jesus and all in him, is mine!
   Alive in him, my living head,
     And clothed in righteousness divine,
   Bold I approach the eternal throne,
   And claim the crown, through Christ my own.

86. Alleluia! Sons of God, arise!

Mimi Armstrong Farra

Refrain
Alleluia! Alleluia!
Alleluia, sons of God, arise.
Alleluia! Alleluia! Sons of God,
Arise and follow the Lord.

1. Come and be clothed in his righteousness;
   Come join the band who are called by his name

2. Look at the world which is bound by sin;
   Walk into the midst of it proclaiming my life.

87. Come and go with me

Anon.

1. Come and go with me to my Father's house,
   to my Father's house, to my Father's house.
   Come and go with me to my Father's house
   where there's joy, joy, joy.

2. It's not very far to my Father's house...

3. There is room for all in my Father's house...

4. Everything is free in my Father's house...

5. Jesus is the way to my Father's house.

6. Jesus is the light in my Father's house

88. Ho! everyone that thirsteth

Isaiah 55: 1-2

Refrain
Ho! everyone that thirsteth, come ye to the waters,
and he that hath no money, come ye, buy and eat.

1. Come, buy without money;
      come, buy without price.
   Come, buy milk and honey
      from Jesus Christ.

2. Wherefore do you spend money
      for that which is not bread;
   and your labour for that which satis-
      -fieth not?

3. Hearken unto me and
      eat that which is good;
   let your soul delight itself in
      fatness, fatness, fatness.

89. The sea walker

Anon.

Take my hand and follow me
To see the sea walker, the blind man healer,
The leper-cleansing man of Galilee.
He's the soul-saver, the one who set me free,
Take my hand and follow me.

90. O Lord, all the world belongs to you

Patrick Appleford

1. O Lord, all the world belongs to you,
    And you are always making all things new.
    What is wrong you forgive, and the new life you
                                                give
    Is what's turning the world upside down.

2. The world's only loving to its friends,
    But your way of loving never ends;
    Loving enemies too, and this loving with you
    Is what's turning the world upside down.

3. This world lives divided and apart;
    You draw men together and we start
    In your body to see that in fellowship we
    Can be turning the world upside down.

4. The world wants the wealth to live in state,
    But you show a new way to be great:
    Like a servant you came, and if we do the same,
    We'll be turning the world upside down.

5. O Lord, all the world belongs to you,
    And you are always making all things new,
    Send your Spirit on all in your Church whom
                                              you call
    To be turning the world upside down.

91. Peace is flowing

Anon.

Peace is flowing like a river,
Flowing out through you and me,
Spreading out into the desert,
Setting all the captives free.

92. God is working his purpose out

Arthur Ainger

1. God is working his purpose out
As year succeeds to year:
God is working his purpose out,
And the time is drawing near;
Nearer and nearer draws the time:
The time that shall surely be,
When the earth shall be filled with the glory of
God
As the waters cover the sea.

2. From utmost east to utmost west.
Where'er man's foot hath trod,
By the mouth of many messengers
Goes forth the voice of God;
Give ear to me, ye continents,
Ye isles, give ear to me,
That the earth may be filled with the glory of God
As the waters cover the sea.

3. March,we forth in the strength of God,
   With the banner of Christ unfurled,
   That the light of the glorious gospel of truth
   May shine throughout the world;
   Fight we the fight with sorrow and sin
   To set their captives free,
   That the earth may be filled with the glory of God
   As the waters cover the sea.

4. All we can do is nothing worth
   Unless God blesses the deed;
   Vainly we hope for the harvest tide
   Till God gives life to the seed;
   Yet nearer and nearer draws the time,
   The time that shall surely be,
   When the earth shall be filled with the glory of
   God

   As the waters cover the sea.

93. Go tell everyone

Alan Dale

1. God's Spirit is in my heart,
      He has called me and set me apart.
    This is what I have to do,
      What I have to do:

Refrain

He sent me to give the good news to the poor,
    Tell prisoners that they are prisoners no more;
Tell blind people that they can see,
    And set the down-trodden free.
And go tell everyone the news that the kingdom of
                                                    God has come,
    And go tell everyone the news that God's kingdom
                                                    has come.

2. Just as the Father sent me
      So I'm sending you out to be
    My witness throughout the world,
      The whole of the world.

3. Don't carry a load in your pack,
      You don't need two shirts on your back,
    A workman can earn his own keep,
      Can earn his own keep.

4. Don't worry what you have to say,
      Don't worry because on that day
    God's Spirit will speak in your heart,
      Will speak in your heart.

94. O Zion, haste

Mary Ann Thompson

1. O Zion, haste, thy mission high fulfilling,
    To tell to all the world that God is light;
That he who made all nations is not willing
    One soul should perish, lost in shades of night:

Refrain
Publish glad tidings: tidings of peace,
   Tidings of Jesus, redemption and release.

2. Proclaim to every people, tongue, and nation
    That God, in whom they live and move, is love;
Tell how he stooped to save his lost creation,
    And died on earth that man might live above.

3. Give of thy sons to bear the message glorious;
    Give of thy wealth to speed them on their way;
Pour out thy soul for them in prayer victorious
    Till God shall bring his kingdom's joyful day.

4. He comes again! O Zion, ere thou meet him,
    Make known to every heart his saving grace;
Let none whom he hath ransomed fail to greet
                                           him,
    Through thy neglect, unfit to see his face.

95. God has spoken

'Song of good news'

W.F.Jabusch

Refrain

God has spoken to his people, hallelujah!
And his words are words of wisdom, hallelujah!

1. Open your ears, O Christian people,
      Open your ears and hear good news.
    Open your hearts, O royal priesthood,
      God has come to you.

2. He who has ears to hear his message,
      He who has ears, then let him hear.
    He who would learn the way of wisdom,
      Let him hear God's word.

3. Israel comes to greet the Saviour;
      Judah is glad to see his day.
    From east and west the peoples travel,
      He will show the way.

96.   # Go forth and tell

J.E.Seddon

1.   Go forth and tell! O Church of God awake!
     God's saving news to all the nations take.
  Proclaim Christ Jesus, Saviour, Lord, and King,
     That all the world his worthy praise may sing.

2.   Go forth and tell! God's love embraces all:
     He will in grace respond to all who call.
  How shall they call if they have never heard
     The gracious invitation of his word?

3.   Go forth and tell! Men still in darkness lie:
     In wealth or want, in sin they live and die.
  Give us, O Lord, concern of heart and mind,
     A love like thine which cares for all mankind.

4.   Go forth and tell! The doors are open wide.
     Share God's good gifts with men so long denied.
  Live out your life as Christ, your Lord, shall
                              choose,
     Your ransomed powers for his sole glory use.

5.   Go forth and tell! O Church of God, arise:
     Go in the strength which Christ your Lord
                              supplies.
  Go, till all nations his great name adore
     And serve him Lord and King for evermore.

97.   Joy in the Lord
(Psalm 100)

Jane Trigg

Refrain
Joy in the Lord,
O be joyful in the Lord,
All ye lands.

1.   Serve the Lord with gladness.
   Come before him with a song.

2.   Be sure the Lord is God.
   He has made us, we are his.

3.   O go into his courts
   With thanksgiving and praise.

4.   Be thankful unto him,
   And speak good of his name.

5.   The Lord is gracious,
   Merciful for evermore.

98. Behold, how good and how pleasant it is
(Psalm 133)

Refrain
Behold how good and how pleasant it is
for brethren to dwell together in unity.

1. It is like the precious ointment upon the head
that ran down upon the beard, even Aaron's
beard,
that ran down to the skirts of his garments;

2. As the dew of Hermon and as the dew
that descended upon the mountain of Zion,
for there the Lord commanded blessing.

3. For there the Lord commanded,
commanded the blessing,
even life for evermore.

99. The Lord has done great things for us

(Psalm 126)

1. When the Lord restored the fortunes of Zion,
   we were like those who dream.
   Then our mouths were filled with laughter,
   and our tongues with shouts of joy!

Refrain
The Lord has done great things for us
   and we are glad.

2. Then they said among the nations,
   'The Lord has done great things for us.'

3. Restore our fortunes, O Lord,
   as the water courses in the Negeb.
   May those who sow in tears,
   reap with shouts of joy!

4. He that goes forth weeping
   bearing the seed for sowing,
   shall come home with shouts of joy,
   bringing his sheaves with him.

100.   The Lord hath put a new song

(Psalm 40)

Mimi Armstrong Farra

Refrain
The Lord hath put a new song in my mouth,
  in my mouth, in my mouth.
The Lord hath put a new song in my mouth,
  even praise unto our God.

1.   And many shall see it and fear and trust,
        fear and trust, fear and trust,
      And many shall see it and fear and trust,
        and shall trust in the Lord.

2.   I delight to do thy will, oh God,
        thy will, oh God, thy will, oh God,
      I delight to do thy will, oh God.
        Thy law is within my heart.

3.   I have not hid thy righteousness within my heart,
        within my heart, within my heart.
      I have not hid thy righteousness within my heart.
        I have declared thy salvation.

4.   I've not concealed thy loving kindness and thy
                                              truth,
        and thy truth, and thy truth,
      I've not concealed thy loving kindness and thy
                                              truth,
        from the great congregation.

5. So let thy loving kindness and thy truth,
      and thy truth, and thy truth,
   so let thy loving kindness and thy truth
      continually preserve me.

6. Let all those that seek thee rejoice and be glad
      rejoice and be glad, rejoice and be glad.
   Let all those that seek thee rejoice and be glad
      rejoice and be glad in thee.

Refrain
The Lord hath put a new song in my mouth,
   in my mouth, in my mouth.
The Lord hath put a new song in my mouth
   even praise unto our God.

101.

As a doe
(Psalm 42)

Mike Fitzgerald

Refrain
As a doe longs for running streams,
so longs my soul for you, my God.

1. My soul is thirsting for the God of life;
        when shall I see him face to face?
   I have no food but tears day and night;
        and men say, 'Where is your God?'

2. I remember and my soul melts within.
        I'm on my way to the house of God,
   among cries of joy and praise;
        place your trust in God.

3. Why so downcast, O my soul?
        Why do you sigh so deep within?
   Place your hope in the God of life.
        I shall praise him again.

4. When I find my soul downcast within,
        I think of you, O mount Zion.
   Deep calls to deep as your waters roar;
        over me all your waves pour.

102.   The Lord's my shepherd
(Psalm 23)

Jessie Seymour Irvine

1.   The Lord's my shepherd, I'll not want;
        He makes me down to lie
     In pastures green; he leadeth me
        The quiet waters by.

2.   My soul he doth restore again;
        And me to walk doth make
     Within the paths of righteousness,
        E'en for his own name's sake.

3.   Yea, though I walk in death's dark vale,
        Yet will I fear none ill:
     For thou art with me; and thy rod
        And staff me comfort still.

4.   My table thou hast furnished
        In presence of my foes;
     My head thou dost with oil anoint,
        And my cup overflows.

5.   Goodness and mercy all my life
        Shall surely follow me:
     And in God's house for evermore
        My dwelling-place shall be.

103. Sing a new song to the Lord
(Psalm 98)

Timothy Dudley-Smith

1. Sing a new song to the Lord,
   He to whom wonders belong!
   Rejoice in his triumph and tell of his power,
   O sing to the Lord a new song!

2. Now to the ends of the earth
   See his salvation is shown!
   And still he remembers his mercy and truth,
   Unchanging in love to his own.

3. Sing a new song and rejoice,
   Publish his praises abroad!
   Let voices in chorus, with trumpet and horn,
   Resound for the joy of the Lord!

4. Join with the hills and the sea
   Thunders of praise to prolong!
   In judgement and justice he comes to the earth,
   O sing to the Lord a new song!

104.   **Bless thou the Lord**

(Psalm 103)

Refrain
Bless thou the Lord, O my soul, *Three times*
and forget not all his benefits.

1.   Who forgiveth all thine iniquities,
          who healeth all thy diseases.

2.   Who redeemeth thy life from destruction,
          who crowneth thee with loving kindness.

3.   The Lord is merciful and gracious,
          slow to anger and plenteous in mercy.

4.   For as the heaven is high above the earth,
          so great his mercy toward them that fear him.

5.   Like as a father pitieth his children,
          so the Lord pitieth them that fear him.

105. I rejoiced when I heard them say
(Psalm 122)

Betty Pulkingham

Refrain
I rejoiced when I heard them say,
    'Let us go to God's house today!'
I rejoiced when I heard them say,
    'Let us go to God's house.'

1. And now our feet are standing,
        standing within thy gates,
    O Jerusalem.

2. Jerusalem is built as a city,
        it is there that the tribes go up,
    the tribes of the Lord.

3. For the peace of Jerusalem pray,
        peace be to your homes,
    Peace to your homes alway.

4. For love of my brethren and friends,
        for love of the house of the Lord,
    I will say, 'Peace, peace upon you.'

After final refrain:
    Let us go to God's house.

106.   The butterfly song

Brian Howard

1.   If I were a butterfly,
        I'd thank you, Lord, for giving me wings.
     And if I were a robin in a tree,
        I'd thank you, Lord, that I could sing.
     And if I were a fish in the sea,
        I'd wiggle my tail and I'd giggle with glee.
     But I just thank you, Father, for making me 'me'.

Refrain
For you gave me a heart and you gave me a smile.
You gave me Jesus and you made me your child.
And I just thank you, Father, for making me 'me'.

2.   If I were an elephant,
        I'd thank you, Lord, by raising my trunk,
     And if I were a kangaroo,
        You know I'd hop right up to you.
     And if I were an octopus,
        I'd thank you, Lord, for my fine looks,
     But I just thank you, Father, for making me 'me'.

3.   If I were a wiggily worm,
        I'd thank you, Lord, that I could squirm.
     And if I were a billy goat
        I'd thank you Lord for my strong throat,
     And if I were a fuzzy-wuzzy bear,
        I'd thank you, Lord, for my fuzzy-wuzzy hair,
     But I just thank you, Father, for making me 'me'.

107.   Jesus, Jesus is my Lord

John Franklin
Age 12

Refrain
Jesus, Jesus is my Lord;
Always obey what Jesus says.

1.   That's the way to lay down your life,
      always obey what Jesus says.
   The ones who come for Jesus' life,
      always obey what Jesus says.

2.   He rewards you, making you free, always...
      And then you have power over the enemy,
                          always...

3.   He has given his Spirit to you, always...
      So keep his words and he will keep you,
                          always...

108. The Lord is my shepherd
(2-part round)

Anon.

The Lord is my shepherd,
   I'll follow him alway.
He leads me by still waters
   I'll follow him alway.
Alway, alway,
   I'll follow him alway.
Alway, alway,
   I'll follow him alway.

109. Oh, how I love Jesus

Refrain: F.Whitfield

Question: Hey, (name) do you love Jesus?
Answer: Yes, I love Jesus.
Q: Are you sure you love Jesus?
A: Yes, I'm sure I love Jesus.
Q: Tell me, why do you love Jesus?
A: This is why I love Jesus,
All: Because he first loved me,
                  Yes, I love him,
               This is why I love him;

Refrain
Oh, how I love Jesus,
Oh, how I love Jesus,
Oh, how I love Jesus,
   Because he first loved me.
All: Yes, I love him, this is why I love him...

110.   **Praise the Lord**

('Sing, sing, praise and sing')

Elizabeth Syré

Refrain
Sing, sing, praise and sing!
Honour God for everything.
Glory to the highest king.
Sing and praise and sing!

1.   Clap your hands, lift your voice,
   Praise the Lord and rejoice!

2.   Full of joy, full of rest,
   In our Lord we are blessed.

3.   Are you weak? Never mind!
   Come and sing, 'God is kind!'

4.   Love and peace is so near.
   Praise the Lord! God can hear!

5.   Cymbal, harp, violin,
   Angels, priests, all join in.

111.   The body song

Betty Pulkingham
Adapted from 1 Cor. 12:14-26

1. If the eye say to the hand, 'I have no need of thee.'
   Or the head to the feet, 'I have no need of you.'
   Well, oh how can we write or hold a thimble?
   How can we walk or run so nimble?
   How can the body be complete without feet?
   How can the body be complete?

2. If the foot shall say, 'Because I'm not the hand,
   I don't feel like a handsome part.'
   Well, oh what does it matter to be first or to be
   latter?
   God has made the body whole and formed
   each part,
   God has made the body whole and formed each
   part.

3. If the ear shall say, 'Because I'm not the eye,
   I don't seem to see things very clearly.'
   Well, oh where were the hearing, and oh where
   were the smelling
   If the whole body were one single eye,
   If the whole body were one eye

4. One single 'I', it cannot be a body.
   One single 'you' a body? 'Nay!'
   Oh, God hath set the members,
   They are many, many members,
   Yet one body as it pleased him are they.
   Yet one body as it pleased him are they.

112.   We love the Lord
(David's song)

David Pulkingham
age 4

We love the Lord,
  Our neighbours and ourselves.
We open our eyes,
  We see him everywhere.
We love the Lord,
  Who died on the cross.
We love the Lord
  To love each other too.
We open our eyes,
  We see Jesus Christ;
He looks down at us,
  We look up at him.
We trust in him
  Eternally.

113. Thank you, Lord

Diane Davis

1. Thank you, Lord, for this fine day, *Three times*
   Right where we are.

Refrain
Alleluia, praise the Lord.
Alleluia, praise the Lord.
Alleluia, praise the Lord,
Right where we are.

2. Thank you, Lord for loving us.

3. Thank you, Lord, for giving us peace.

4. Thank you, Lord, for setting us free.

5. Thank you, Lord, for games to play.

114. Jesus is a friend of mine

Paul Mazak
age 4

1. Jesus is a friend of mine,
      Praise him.
    Jesus is a friend of mine,
      Praise him.
    Praise him, praise him.
    Jesus is a friend of mine,
      Praise him.

2. Jesus died to set us free,
      Praise him.

3. He gave us the victory,
      Praise him.

4. Jesus is the King of kings,
      Praise him.

115.   The wedding banquet

Miriam Therese Winter

Refrain
I cannot come.
I cannot come to the banquet, don't trouble me now.
 I have married a wife, I have bought me a cow.
I have fields and commitments that cost a pretty sum.
 Pray, hold me excused, I cannot come.

1.   A certain man held a feast on his fine estate in
                                                town,
        He laid a festive table and wore a wedding
                                                gown.
        He sent invitations to his neighbours far and
                                                wide,
        But when the meal was ready, each of them
                                                replied:

2.   The master rose up in anger, called his servants
                                                by name,
        Said: 'Go into the town, fetch the blind and the
                                                lame,
        Fetch the peasant and the pauper, for this I have
                                                willed,
        My banquet must be crowded, and my table
                                                must be filled.'

3. When all the poor had assembled, there was still
                                    room to spare,
    So the master demanded: 'Go search everywhere,
    To the highways and the byways, and force them
                                    to come in.
    My table must be filled before the banquet can
                                    begin.'

4. Now God has written a lesson for the rest of man-
                                    kind;
    If we're slow in responding, he may leave us
                                    behind.
    He's preparing a banquet for that great and
                                    glorious day.
    When the Lord and Master calls us, be certain
                                    not to say:

116.   Wake up!

Betty Pulkingham

Refrain

Wake up! Wake up! It's time to rise and sing the
praise of Jesus,
Allelu, alleluia.
It's time to rise, to sing, to shout, to bring him all your
heart.
He'll do the bigger part, if you will only make a start.

1. In the days of Noah's family,
The people didn't know what the score was
eternally.
They ate, and drank, got married and then
Their sons and their daughters did the same
things again.

2. John came baptising in the wilderness;
Preaching to those who their sins confessed.
But to those who came for strife and debate, he
said,
'Who told you to come here, you tribe of
snakes!'

3. When Jesus came to John in the wilderness;
John said, 'I should be the one to come to you,
I must confess!
For I baptise with water at the most,
But you will baptise with the Holy Ghost!'

4. Jesus told a story of ten maidens fair;
Five were wise and ready, five did not prepare.
Those girls had lamps, but oh, dear me!
They had no oil to light them so that they
could see.

5.   What good is a lamp without any oil?
       What good is our life if we struggle and toil,
    But cannot see God's kingdom here,
       And live the loving life of his Son so dear?

117.   On Jordan's bank

Charles Coffin
Tr. John Chandler

1.   On Jordan's bank the Baptist's cry
      Announces that the Lord is nigh;
   Awake and hearken, for he brings
      Glad tidings of the King of kings.

2.   Then cleansed be every breast from sin;
      Make straight the way for God within,
   And let each heart prepare a home
      Where such a mighty guest may come.

3.   For thou art our salvation, Lord,
      Our refuge, and our great reward;
   Without thy grace we waste away
      Like flowers that wither and decay.

4.   To heal the sick stretch out thine hand,
      And bid the fallen sinner stand;
   Shine forth, and let thy light restore
      Earth's own true loveliness once more.

5.   All praise, eternal Son, to thee,
      Whose advent doth thy people free;
   Whom with the Father we adore
      And Holy Ghost for evermore.

118. Calypso carol

Michael Perry

1. See him a'lying on a bed of straw;
   Draughty stable with an open door,
   Mary cradling the babe she bore;
   The prince of glory is his name.

Refrain
   Oh, now carry me to Bethlehem
   To see the Lord appear to men;
   Just as poor as was the stable then,
   The prince of glory when he came.

2. Star of silver sweep across the skies,
   Show where Jesus in the manger lies.
   Shepherds swiftly from your stupor rise
   To see the Saviour of the world.

3. Angels, sing again the song you sang,
   Bring God's glory to the heart of man;
   Sing that Bethl'hem's little baby can
   Be salvation to the soul.

4. Mine are riches from thy poverty,
   From thine innocence, eternity;
   Mine, forgiveness by thy death for me,
   Child of sorrow for my joy.

119.   Oh, Mary, don't you weep

Mimi Armstrong Farra

Refrain
Oh, Mary don't you weep,
And Mary don't you cry.

1. Oh, little baby Jesus,
     Baby Jesus is gonna die, but...

2. Baby Jesus is gonna die,
     Gonna die that we might live for ever.

3. Oh, sing glory hallelujah,
     Glory, glory baby Jesus.

120.   **See, amid the winter's snow**

Edward Caswall

1.   See amid the winter's snow,
     Born for us on earth below
   See the tender Lamb appears,
     Promised from eternal years.

Refrain
Hail, thou ever-blessed morn!
Hail redemption's happy dawn!
Sing through all Jerusalem:
Christ is born in Bethlehem.

2.   Lo, within a manger lies
     He who built the starry skies,
   He who throned in height sublime,
     Sits amid the cherubim.

3.   Say, ye holy shepherds, say,
     What your joyful news today;
   Wherefore have ye left your sheep
     On the lonely mountain steep?

4.   'As we watched at dead of night,
     Lo, we saw a wondrous light:
   Angels, singing peace on earth,
     Told us of the Saviour's birth.

5.   Sacred infant, all divine,
     What a tender love was thine,
   Thus to come from highest bliss
     Down to such a world as this!

6.   Teach, O teach us, holy child,
     By thy face so meek and mild,
   Teach us to resemble thee
     In thy sweet humility.

121. Go tell it on the mountain

North American spiritual

Refrain
Go tell it on the mountain,
   Over the hills and everywhere.
Go tell it on the mountain
   That Jesus Christ is born.

1. While shepherds kept their watching
      O'er silent flocks by night.
   Behold throughout the heavens
      There shone a holy light.

2. The shepherds feared and trembled
      When lo, above the earth
   Rang out the angel chorus
      That hailed the Saviour's birth.

3. Down in a lowly manger
      Our humble Christ was born,
   And God sent us salvation
      That blessed Christmas morn.

4. When I was a seeker,
      I sought both night and day;
   I asked the Lord to help me,
      And he showed me the way.

5. He made me a watchman
      Upon the city wall,
   And if I am a Christian,
      I am the least of all.

122. Let your light shine

Shirley Lewis Brown

1. Let your light shine,
     Let your light shine,
   Let your light shine before men,
   That they may see,
     May see your good works,
   And glorify the Father,
     The Father,
   The Father who is in heaven.

2. Once there was darkness,
     Once there was darkness,
   Once there was darkness upon earth.
   Then God sent Jesus,
     Then God sent Jesus
   To light the way, the pathway,
     The pathway,
   The pathway back to God.

3. What did he tell us?
     What did he tell us?
   What did he tell us we should do?
   He said to love God,
     To love your neighbour,
   And serve him; let your light shine,
     Let your light shine,
   Let your light shine before men.

123.   Wondrous love

Trad.

1.   What wondrous love is this, O my soul, O my
soul?
What wondrous love is this, O my soul?
What wondrous love is this that caused the Lord
of bliss
To bear the dreadful curse for my soul, for my
soul,
To bear the dreadful curse for my soul.

2.   When I was sinking down, sinking down, sinking
down,
When I was sinking down, sinking down,
When I was sinking down beneath God's right-
eous frown,
Christ laid aside his crown for my soul, for my
soul,
Christ laid aside his crown for my soul.

3.   To God and to the Lamb I will sing, I will sing
To God and to the Lamb I will sing.
To God and to the Lamb who is the great I AM,
While thousands join the theme, I will sing, I will
sing,
While thousands join the theme, I will sing.

4.   And when from death I'm free, I'll sing on, I'll
sing on,
And when from death I'm free, I'll sing on.
And when from death I'm free, I'll sing and
joyful be,
And through eternity I'll sing on, I'll sing on,
And through eternity I'll sing on.

124.   The King of glory

W.F.Jabusch

Refrain
The King of glory comes,
The nation rejoices.
Open the gates before him,
Lift up your voices.

1. Who is the King of glory; how shall we call him?
   He is Emmanuel, the promised of ages.

2. In all of Galilee, in city or village,
   He goes among his people curing their illness.

3. Sing then of David's son, our Saviour and brother;
   In all of Galilee was never another.

4. He gave his life for us, the pledge of salvation.
   He took upon himself the sins of the nation.

5. He conquered sin and death; he truly has risen,
   And he will share with us his heavenly vision.

125.   The foot washing song

Shirley Lewis-Brown
Adapted from John 13

Refrain
Put on the apron of humility;
Serve your brother, wash his feet,
That he may walk in the way of the Lord,
Refreshed, refreshed.

1. At the last supper with his disciples Jesus rose
   from the table,
   took a towel and a basin of water and stooped to
   wash their feet.

2. When Jesus knelt before him, Peter said, 'Lord,
   do you wash my feet?'
   Jesus answered, 'Now you don't understand, but
   later on you will.'
   Still protesting, Peter said, 'Lord, you must never
   wash my feet.'
   Jesus answered, 'If I don't wash you, you have no
   part of me.'

3. Then said Peter, 'Lord, not only my feet, but also
   my hands and my head.'
   Jesus answered, 'He who has washed need only
   wash his feet.'

4. Then said Jesus, 'Do you know what it is that I
   have done?
   You call me your master and Lord, and you
   speak the truth, for so I am.
   If I then, your master and Lord, have stooped to
   wash your feet,
   So ought you men also to wash the feet of one
   another.'

5. No man is greater than his master, no messenger
   than he who sent him.
   If you men know these things then happy are you
   if you do them.'

126. Were you there?

North American spiritual

1. Were you there when they crucified my Lord?
    Oh! Sometimes it causes me to tremble, tremble,
    tremble.
    Were you there when they crucified my Lord?

2. Were you there when they nailed him to the
    tree?
    Oh! Sometimes it causes me to tremble, tremble,
    tremble.
    Were you there when they nailed him to the
    tree?

3. Were you there when they laid him in the tomb?
    Oh! Sometimes it causes me to tremble, tremble,
    tremble.
    Were you there when they laid him in the tomb?

127.   I am the resurrection

Ray Repp

Refrain
I am the resurrection and the life;
He who believes in me will never die.
I am the resurrection and the life;
He who believes in me will live a new life.

1.   I have come to bring the truth;
   I have come to bring you life;
   If you believe, then you shall live.

2.   In my word all men will come to know
   It is love which makes the spirit grow.
   If you believe, then you shall live.

3.   Keep in mind the things that I have said;
   Remember me in the breaking of the bread.
   If you believe then you shall live.

128. Thine be the glory

Edmond Louis Budry
Tr. Richard Birch Hoyle

1. Thine be the glory, risen conquering Son,
Endless is the victory thou o'er death hast won;
Angels in bright raiment rolled the stone away,
Kept the folded grave-clothes, where thy body
lay.

Refrain
Thine be the glory, risen, conquering Son,
Endless is the victory thou o'er death hast won!

2. Lo, Jesus meets us, risen, from the tomb!
Lovingly he greets us, scatters fear and gloom:
Let the church with gladness hymns of triumph
sing,
For her Lord now liveth, death hath lost its sting.

3. No more we doubt thee, glorious prince of life;
Life is nought without thee: aid us in our strife;
Make us more than conquerors, through thy
deathless love;
Bring us safe through Jordan to thy home above.

129 & 130. Christ the Lord is risen today

Charles Wesley

1. Christ the Lord is risen today: Hallelujah!
      Sons of men and angels say, 'Hallelujah!'
    Raise your joys and triumphs high: Hallelujah!
      Sing ye heavens; thou earth reply, Hallelujah!

2. Love's redeeming work is done; Hallelujah!
      Fought the fight, the battle won, Hallelujah!
    Death in vain forbids him rise, Hallelujah!
      Christ hath opened paradise, Hallelujah!

3. Lives again our glorious King! Hallelujah!
      Where, O death, is now thy sting? Hallelujah!
    Once he died our souls to save, Hallelujah!
      Where thy victory, O grave? Hallelujah!

4. Soar we now where Christ has led, Hallelujah!
      Following our exalted Head; Hallelujah!
    Made like him, like him we rise; Hallelujah!
      Ours the cross, the grave, the skies; Hallelujah!

131.   He will fill your hearts today

Refrain: Mrs. C.H. Morris
Verses: Betty Pulkingham

Refrain
He will fill your hearts today to overflowing,
As the Lord commanded you
    'Bring your vessels not a few,'
He will fill your hearts today to overflowing
    With his Holy Ghost and power.

1.   When the day of Pentecost had come,
        The believers were gathered together,
        Were gathered together in one place,
            Of one mind as the Lord had commanded.

2.   Suddenly a noise from the sky,
        Which sounded like a strong wind blowing,
        A strong wind blowing by,
            Filled the whole place, the noise kept on
                                        growing.

3.   Then they looked up and saw,
        They saw what looked like tongues of fire,
        Tongues of fire spreading out,
            To each one, spreading out to all the people.

4.   All of them were filled with the Holy Ghost,
        With the Holy Ghost and power.
        They began to speak in other languages,
            In other languages he gave them in that hour!

132.   Come, Holy Ghost

Trad.

1.   Come, Holy Ghost creator blest,
      Vouchsafe within our souls to rest;
    Come with thy grace and heavenly aid,
      And fill the hearts which thou hast made,
    And fill the hearts which thou hast made.

2.   To thee the comforter we cry;
      To thee the gift of God most high;
    The fount of life, the fire of love,
      The soul's anointing from above.

3.   The sevenfold gifts of grace are thine,
      O finger of the hand divine.
    True promise of the Father thou,
      Who dost the tongue with speech endow.

4.   Thy light to every sense impart,
      And shed thy love in every heart;
    Thine own unfailing might supply,
      To strengthen our infirmity.

5.   Drive far away our ghostly foe,
      And thine abiding peace bestow;
    If thou be our preventing guide,
      No evil can our steps betide.

133.　　　　Planted wheat

Jeff Cothran

1. Planted wheat, within the wheatfields,
   waiting till the summer time is near.
   Growing wheat, above the ploughlands,
   showing that the Lord of lords is here.

Refrain
He comes to grow a new creation, calling out a holy
nation,
   all who will believe, and all who will receive.

2. Jesus rose, we cannot see him;
   he is seated at the Father's hand.
   Yet he walks within his harvest,
   men in love obeying his command.

3. Jesus Christ is Lord of the harvest.
   Soon in glory he will come again,
   Bringing all his holy angels,
   gathering in the ripened sheaves of grain.

Index of Titles and First Lines

The first line of a song is included, in italic type, only where it differs from the title.

Authors and Copyright Owners

Greenwood, Pamela. 54; © 1974, Pamela Greenwood.

Harmon, Bill. 39; © 1958, Gospel Publishing House. All rights reserved. Used by permission.

Head, B.P. 43; © 1951, Mrs. B.P. Head.

Howard, Brian. 8, © 1974; 61, © 1973; 106, © 1974, The Fishermen, Inc. Used by permission.

Iverson, Daniel. 29; © 1935, 1963. Moody Press, Moody Bible Institute of Chicago. Used by permission.

Jabusch, W.F. 95,124; By permission W.F. Jabusch.

Kerner, Debby. 57; © 1973, Maranatha! Music, ASCAP All rights reserved. International copyright secured. Used by permission.

Krieger, Jacob. 84; © 1973, The Word of God. P.O.Box 87, Ann Arbor, MI 48107, U.S.A. All rights reserved. Used by permission.

Lafferty, Karen. 58; © 1973, Marantha! Music, ASCAP All rights reserved. International copyright secured. Used by permission.

Lawton, Sylvia. 32; © 1974, Sylvia Lawton. Used by permission.

Mansell, David. 82; © 1971, David Mansell. Used by permission.

Mazak, Paul. 114; © 1974, The Fishermen, Inc. Used by permission.

Morris, Mrs. C.H. 131; © 1912, renewal 1940, F.M. Lunk. Assigned to Hope Publishing Co. All rights reserved. Used by permission.

Owens, Jimmy. 19; © 1972, Lexicon Music, Inc. From the musical 'Come together'. All rights reserved. International copyright secured. Used by special permission.

Perry, Michael. 118; © 1969, M. Perry & S. Coates. Used by permission.

Peterson, J.W. 77; © 1950, Singspiration, Inc. All rights reserved. Used by permission

Pulkingham, Betty. 77, © 1971; 111, © 1971; 116, © 1972; 131, verses; © 1971, The Fishermen, Inc. Used by permission.